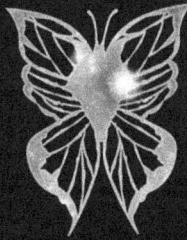

Butterfly Kisses

By
Salima Mansouri

Published by True Beginnings Publishing.
Copyright 2017.

True Beginnings Publishing

Dedication

To the man of my life; the protector, the lover, the most amazing father, Muhamed Mansouri.

To the woman who raised me up to be me, and I am proud of who I am because of her; my wonderful mother, Jiji Mansouri.

You Both, for your smile, I came up with this book.

Thanks to everyone who believed in me. Thanks even to who thought of this butterfly can't fly far away. I thank them sincerely.

For them I showed I could fly and would always rise…

Love you all with butterfly kisses.

Introduction

"A woman's intuitive nature leads her to a direct opening from heart to mind. Whenever love is within that midst, she breathes a loving flora into her space. Salima, both beautiful and strong, knows exactly where her heart strings are tied. She delivers in her quotes, not only about life, an array of beauty that's dug so deeply inside of love. Her writings are not too common, but arranged in a way that everyone seems to relate. Her recounts with love, its feelings, and the surreal impact it delivers is all expressed upon the pages. Sometimes when falling out of love, we forget its true beauty and oh what a lovely collage Salima seems to paint for us to remember. Her written language is soft and delicate, sweet and stunning, while encouraging our hearts to reminisce. To stimulate our emotions, she voices carefully an urge within that we all just can't seem to let pass by. It's romantic, its prose on petals, softs and silky words that we all felt or would love to feel. This book is simply what you've been waiting for to take you back to that place where love was so tender and flowing, like honey."

Shantelle 'Elle' McLin (USA)
Author~Mentor~Philospher~Photographer

Reviews

"With this book, *Butterfly Kisses*, The flowery gate of your heart will open, reflecting the light and shadow of your very essence. It bares your fears, your desires, and your beauty that you may have never known before. Be prepared to go through a true life maze and come out with unexpected joy!"

Cordie Aquino (Florida. USA)

"*Butterfly Kisses* is an insightful, authentic and transformative book. The eye-opening messages which are packed into its pages can draw all spiritual lovers to a path of challenge and growth if they open their hearts to their lucid wisdom. Salima Mansouri shares with us valuable insights on our ability to experience the beauty that lies in the depth of the self. Any age reader can use her ideas of love to access their inner drive and find the empowerment they need to both live authentically and achieve real lasting happiness."

Maria Bechlivanidou (Thessaloniki, Greece)

"Words are mere words if the poetry doesn't speak with passion and stir the heart and soul like love does. Your words speak with passion and stir hearts and souls, Salima."

Lourdes Alexander (Mumbai, India)

"Her poems, Butterflies in flight... Illuminating thousands... shadows of our souls and love."

Diana Nicolle (Negoita, Bucharest, Romania)

"Salima is a beautiful soul whose gift for poetry is fueled by her passion for life. She has this gift of eloquence as she finds just the right words to the feelings most of us cannot speak. Her works mostly focus on the beauty of love and positivity that it will always leave you feeling enlightened and hopeful in the end. Truly a poetess to watch for."

Candice Angeli (Iloilo City, the Philippines)

"Salima touches with the soul and sees with the heart... speaks with mastery of the magnetic force of Love... There is a harmonic resonance, a unification between poetry and the most fundamental level of Being, the level of the Divine Spark, the subatomic level, which precedes any organization of physical form..."

Ivone Lopes Mascarenhas Caxambu (Minas Gerais, Brasil)

"Salima, your writing is Anglican; full of soul, depth and Love. The beauty of your writing is beyond words to discribe... You touched my heart with the first sentence that I've ever read from you. You're my inspiration and for everyone that is blessed with having the opportunity to read and feel what you are saying."

Nadia Garbaui (Roosendaal, the Netherlands)

"Salima, the words are not enough to express the way your writings make me feel. You have this unique gift to touch my soul with every single line that you write! It is with your soul that you write and that makes it impossible to not touch other people's soul in return. I feel blessed for having the opportunity to read your writings!"

Atalanta Gjylkaj (Athens, Greece)

Who Am I?

I was a caterpillar… An impatient dreamer of having wings so I could fly here and there. I fought in my cocoon to see the light of the moon. I fell and rose in darkness and light. I pushed and pushed to change. I strived to force my head out to face the light and live in love. I slipped so many times, but all that matters is I am rising now as a beautiful butterfly, kissing the dew on the flowers in my garden 'til my sun shines and I will keep rising…

Salima Mansouri

I believe a pen comes to life and lives its purpose when it is held by a good writer. It will make miracles by changing people's worlds with a person's words.

She ignited the thread of Love in her waxen life.
She wants to be free.
She wants a life.
As the fire in her love grows, the life that imprisoned her
light vanishes in the flames.
She shared her flame to enlighten a million like her.
Her light can never be diminished.

There is no better company that comes to a better understanding of self like the company of you and yourself.

Strengthen your self-relationship by taking yourself on a journey to your soul.

Talk.
Walk.
Care about being there.
Enjoy your you.
Water what has wilted in you.

Let the sun peek in to perk up the love for yourself at its roots. Then watch your inner you grow and blossom like Love.

When life tries to take her to her breaking point,
she smiles and bends with it.

She is unbreakable.
She is woman.

Life is beautiful. It will always treat you as you treat it; gives you back what you give it. This is why I chose to smile at it, so it smiles back at me.

If life throws stones at you, throw back flowers.
Life will soften up and smile at you.

I was wrong when I summed up love and life in a short song.

'Til I met you.

Then I recognized that love and life are mixed up in a long beautiful song, that has no end when you are singing the lyrics.

Stop looking for Love!
Be Love, and Love will find you.

The change doesn't occur where you begin, or where you end. It is the leaps of faith in between that change your life. So, make sure your jump is worth the risk.

When I whispered Love, only Love could hear me.
Love loves me. I love my love with all of me.

Life was miserable by itself 'til it met Love.
As they spent more time together, as they bonded,
they came to understand the wholeness of oneness.

It started with you—with a word—then I made you
and that word my world.

She chose to stay in the light because it fit her.
Darkness only enhanced the light of love in her.

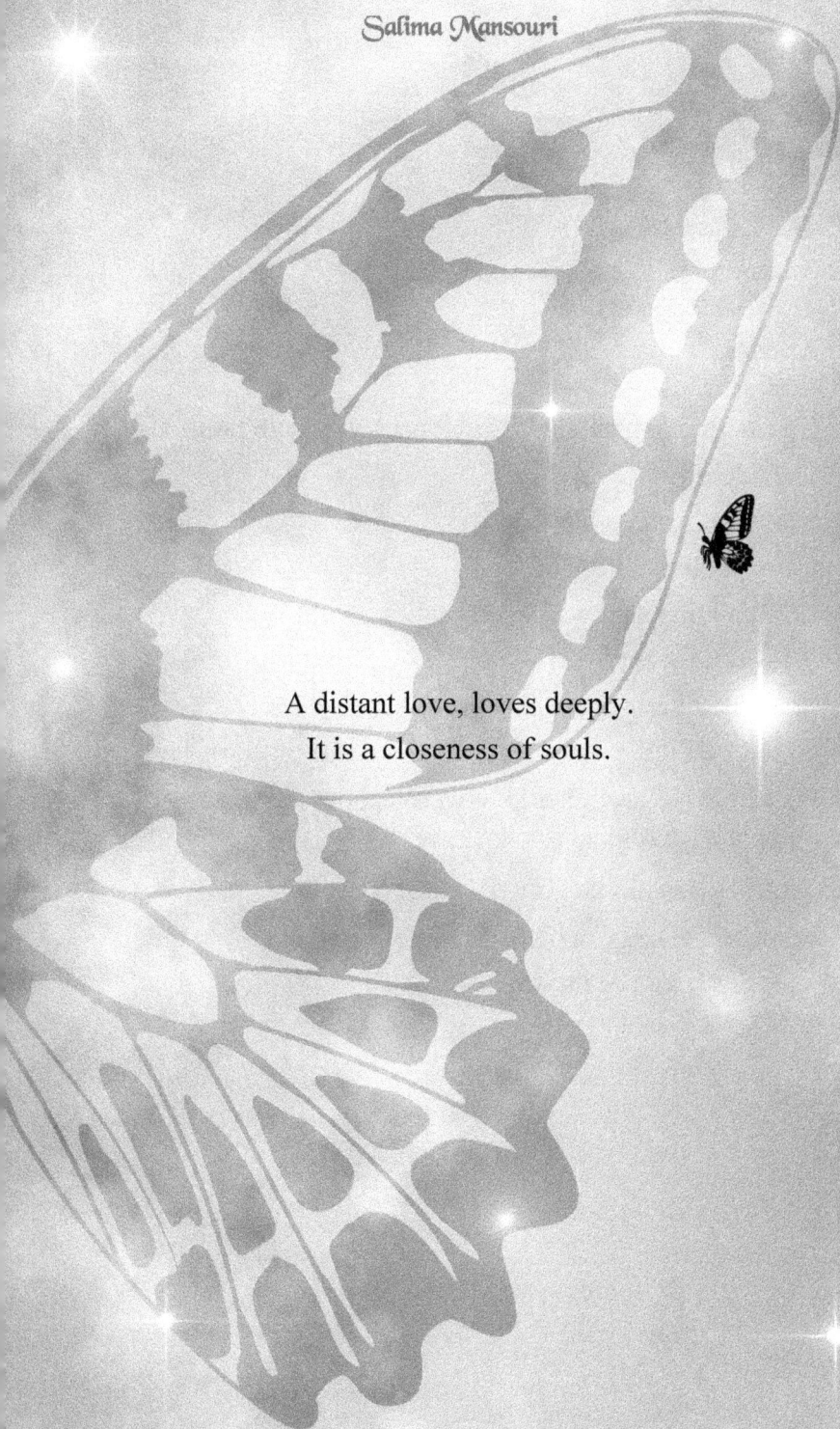

A distant love, loves deeply.
It is a closeness of souls.

He caught her hand and invited her to fly with him.

She asked to where?!

Shhh! He stroked her hair.

Come with me, he said.

Love is blind as it was said.

With you I want to go ahead.

She raised her head

and moved on!

He wanted to teach her love wasn't about words to be said.

Or someone to be led.

True Love walks silently,

because it takes you by itself to your destiny.

Only Love knows its way.

You kissed my heart with the first "I love you".
Your words gently caressed my mind, then I
couldn't stop thinking of you. You embraced the
feelings in me, and you made love to my soul.
You gave life to this love I have for you.

You entered my heart without permission, because
it was already yours.

Her body had imprisoned her soul long enough;
now she wanted a love to free her forever.
He gave her that love.
She gave him the key to her all.

What occurs in life doesn't matter as much as who stands beside us in all ways. A queen balances her king and vice versa.

What happened to us is that our souls crossed miles to live the oneness of togetherness, so they could feel their wholeness.

Take her by the hand. Fly with her to La La land.
Remind her of how beautiful she is. Tell her love
stories. Love is not a mere word. Love is to make
her feel she is loved. Love is to make her your
world.

I don't want to just be closer to you;

I want to be a part of you.

Give me all of you to blend all of me with.

Pull me into your soul.

Let me feel the warmth of it.

Let me singe my lips from the flames of your kiss and the
fire in your passion.

All in one as one.

Let's burn together.

We could never end or vanish completely.

Our love is eternal.

Even our dust will forever carry the fragrance of love on
the winds.

Let's burn together in this Love, my love.

True Love is a language that only lovers can speak. It can be understood only by those who put all of themselves into keeping it alive.

Whenever she missed him, clouds were moved by the
breeze of the sweet bitter missing, pushed by her fiery soul
and passion. To settle on his place and rain over his head.

It wasn't rain.
They were tears of her, calling upon him.
Crying over him.
Eagering for the oneness.
Calling for the togetherness.

He heard and felt. He wiped her tears mixed up with his.
And the sun rose in her place over her head. She smiled
and the joy overwhelmed her heart. She knew that was a
sign they will meet eventually. As the sun rose, their souls
shone and rejoiced.

She didn't have a reason to love him. She only loved him without expectations. She walked aimlessly in his love. Darkness covered his soul, but with light in her she could walk in, trying to make changes in his weary, hopeless spirit.

She took his heart gently and caressed so he feels her warmth. He slowly did. He never felt such a peace within. He pulled her to him because he adapted to change. He wanted her to stay in forever. She could enlighten his soul again after the hurt he was in. She always believed in darkness could only enhance the light. She was light.

She was clear in her intentions because she didn't have anything to hide. She wasn't asking for a life from him. She wanted to make him her life, as he had made her his. She didn't want to hear the word "freedom" from others, because freedom for her was to love him freely with her entirety.

She had been a caterpillar
She dreamed of having beautiful wings-
Wander joyfully in a fairyland.
She wanted to place kisses
On the flowers of her garden
Each and every morning
As the dew was kissed away
By the sun.
She wanted to sow happiness
And delight all who would see
Wherever her footprints lit the petals
Softly,
Gently.
And she grew to be a wonderful butterfly
With wings like rainbow's colors
But those wings she had waited eagerly for
Took her nowhere at all
She could not gladly wander through the blossoms
Perhaps because her dreams
Were bigger than her little wings.

Come with me to this way…
It is not done. It has just begun.

He loves me like I love him.
When we sing our songs of love,
we watch the dancing of birds above.
We compose beautiful songs together;
we are the melody, and our love is the music.

He is the love in me.
He is the passion in me.
He is my sunshine.
He is the light in me.
He is the life in me.
I love him with all of me.

Don't look at me. Look through me.
I am not the face. I am the essence I embrace.

Your eyes were the bridge to my love.
My heart had been wandering, seeking the perfect love for
   me. The light in you guided me.
I knocked on your beautiful heart with tender intentions.
It had been out in the cold, so I covered it with my soul so
   you would feel the warmth of my love for you.
The love in you awakened, shaken from a deep sleep.
It reached for me.
It cuddled me.
It didn't want me to leave its embrace.
Looking in each other's eyes,
Our love breathed the first breath of life.
A new life was born in me with the first deep look into
   your eyes.
I am born again every time you look at me, my love.

Far but close to me,

Your love aroused me;

Awakened me.

A love touch I feel.

A soul match I live.

Over me you always watch.

I feel your hand catch mine when I think of you.

Each breath says I miss you.

Each heartbeat tells I love you.

In the words "I love you" there is still too much distance.

That is why I say "I live you".

In a world she was not familiar with…

a beautiful world…

He laid her gently in his love and spoke poetry to her soul.

In a lasting love scene, he awakened such enticing
feelings.

He whispered… "I am here, Baby.

With you.

In you.

Never let this love leave its home.

It lives here.

Where we live.

Where we belong."

She wrapped herself with his love.

Cuddled in her feelings, she answered his poetry with
    poetry of her own...
"I feel you, Baby.
Stay in here.
This is where you are meant to be.
Here with me.
I am never letting you go.
You are my soul."

You unlocked my heart before you got to whisper "I love you". Your eyes were the key to my love. And because it happened in a blink of an eye, I tried to catch my heart, but I found my soul was already there with you.

I left my soul with you after the first "I love you".

They have separate perspectives of life, but one word gathers them together, and that is "LOVE".

Life tells stories. Love lives them.

It wasn't about how she looked. He loved her deeply because he listened to her first. He gave her wings to fly after she was a caterpillar. She became a beautiful butterfly. She left her cocoon to settle on his heart so he gets to listen to her constantly. While she plays on his heartstrings his favorite songs, his mind repeats the lyrics, and his soul dances on the scenes of the beautiful life she gave him.

It is amazing to be with someone who will count the stars in a dark sky with you on lonely nights, then point to the moon to show the beauty in darkness. All while waiting for the sun to peak the horizon, to see the beauty in a bright new day.

I embraced YOU in ME, then I looked for ME to find YOU, YOU took all of ME.

She walked carefully around the edge of his heart, because she didn't want to step on the wounds others had left. He was hurt enough. The healing peace of the love prints she left as she walked into his soul soothed the hurt away. He pulled her deeper within him and made her his everything.

He had crossed the miles of the sea of love, crashing into rocks. He was about to give up, thinking he couldn't be saved, when a wave of love came from afar, yet from a close place. It cradled him tenderly and pulled him safely to a peaceful shore.

He composed for her beautiful new love songs to play on
   her ears.
Music she had never heard before.
He had to tell her how beautiful she was in a thousand
   different ways.
He thought it was her ego speaking more loudly than her
   heart in a selfish way.
But he saw it was not that.
She was different.
She deserved something new to hear.
And not just a shiny diamond ring on her finger from
   anyone of the same old sad singers.
She had no desire to clean the dust off of their lyrics.
She didn't want him to take her hand and lead her to dance
   to the old songs with the tired words that had been
   sung for others.
She wanted to be appreciated for her uniqueness.
This is how she was.
She refused to be a million other women, like the ones
   who gladly, blindly danced the dance like that.
And that's what made her the only woman for him in all of
   that.

Her body wasn't his destination. It was only a map to reach her soul. He followed the beating of her heart until he found it. There was a door there with a bright light behind it. He opened it and stepped deeper to her essence. His pure intentions felt like sweet caresses. He sat down by the fire so they could live in the light of each other's fire forever.

She doesn't have to wonder or read implicitly
between the words to know what he has for her.
He has to be clear, because Love doesn't come with
interpretations; as it doesn't need him to choose
fancy words to reach her heart. Feelings are pure.
They are transparent. He just needs to say the
words in a way she feels, and give her his all, so
she can feel comfortable in doing the same.

She was the peaceful love he had dreamed to have one day. She was familiar to him because he had seen her in his dreams. She was his rainbow that signaled the end of his rainy days. She was his sunshine, his new day. He woke up and she was no longer a dream. Now she is the real love he lives in every day.

He lives between the lines of my poetry. My words and feelings for him are endless, ageless. Every breath I take in his love, I am reborn over and over again. He is the poem. My poem.

Despair and weakness upon her
She walked in the midst of darkness
Alone she walked
Blindly
Aimlessly
She lost her destination
Did not know where to go
Her soul in pain she cried out
And reached for him.
He heard her cry-
Felt her pain.
Gently, he spoke to her soul;
Only her heart could hear
Those words.
Those thoughts sent from afar
Comforted her, and she understood
That what she sought, she already had.
He was part of her.

He lives in her breath-
Lingers in her soul.
His love runs in her veins,
Shining a light for her alone.
She gazed out at life again'
As he filled her with hope,
And she felt peace in her soul again,
For he is ever closer
Than the miles between them.
His touch inside her
Was her torch.

She walked miles on the sands of life, leaving footprints of
    love wherever she went.
He saw her from afar.
There were only her footprints to follow.
He thought she was gone.
But he felt her steps on his heart walking carefully around
    the edge of his love.
That was her path to linger into the depth of his soul.
She never wanted to be his part, but his all.
She flamed the love's fire to burn her soul into his, to be
    his oneness. Wholeness.

The love dust fragranced out.
They scattered the ash everywhere.
Their love's flame could never be extinguished.
And then they celebrated the birth of their love over and
    over again.
It was eternal.

She told her love story to the moon, for only it understands the meaning of what it means to be full. She is full of love for him. When she thinks of him, butterflies float around her. She wishes she had their wings to fly her to him, so she can stop wishing upon a star and be home with him. Their love seems like a dream, and she may be a dreamer, but she is an even stronger lover.

Next to you, I can hear my heart's palpitations…

Next to you, I have no time for expectations…

Next to you, the sea is an ink I hold my pen, dive
    into my sea…

And in writing about your love, I sink.

Next to you, the world is mine.

Because with you I feel I can control thrones and
    reign. I can be this and that only with you, so
    keep me next to you.

Sorry, Baby, I never told you what I loved about you because I loved you before I ever had to. I loved you before I expected where this love would take me. And I loved you before I knew you.

How do I love you? I have no one reason I love you. I love the feeling of your presence in your absence. I love how I feel my heartbeats when I feel your soul's existence. I love how you touch my mind and have me thinking of you all the time. I love the caress of your soul moving through mine. I love you because I have always loved you. Ever since you rubbed your heart against mine to set this love aflame. The fire from our first kiss gave birth to this love as if it were a phoenix rising from the fire.

Don't wait for happiness to come knock on your door. Open your door and go to it. Make a truce with the impediment that is laying across your path, stagnating your progress in life.

She dreamed and waited for him to catch her hand and walk together slowly into the altar. She didn't want only a bridal gown, but what comes after. She said her vow many times in front of the mirror. She promised to make him happy and satisfied. Music was turned on. She put a step to walk on her favorite song, but she waited for so long. 'Til she felt there was something wrong. He never came. He left her next to the mirror dreaming of a walk that takes them together to forever. But she was a dreamer.

He asked: "Let me linger in you."

She replied: "I have a fire inside."

He asked: "Let me in. I want to feel your warmth."

She replied: "I am afraid you would burn."

Moving closer to her and whispered: "I want to burn to
   ashes in you. Let me in."

She came to him as a storm, forcing him to adapt to change. Her love in him was a volcano erupting and bringing out the best in him. She was a tornado, twisting and pulling his heart into hers. And she was his earthquake, shaking the buried love from his soul to have his love be unearthed and visible to her forever. Her love was a force of nature.

Singe your lips in the fire of mine. Kiss
passionately my soul and hug it tightly. Caress my
heart, then rub it to yours. Let's burn. Let's vanish
'til our remains smoke love. Keep doing it over and
over 'til our souls declare the oneness. The
wholeness.

He cleared the dust on her weary soul. He revealed who she is. Before him she was a fiction, a shadow, a shallow thought. His love created her all over again. He brought out the beauty and the light from the depths of her shadowy soul to show her she could never again be like she was. The feeling of having him, having that someone there freeing her soul from the bonds of a hurtful past, brought tears of joy to her eyes.

She wanted to fly with him to the unknown. She
didn't want to think where that would take her or
what it would cost her. She wondered which she
should follow: her heart or her mind. In the fight
between love and reason, she emerged between
both polarities and chose to walk slowly with her
soul to her destiny. And it is still an unknown
destination.

Each moment he passes by her mind, she feels the caresses of his peaceful thoughts. She loses her breaths in every step to gather them again in every tender thought of him. He haunted her mind peacefully. But that wasn't enough for him. He walked in her veins to reside in her heart carefully. She felt him, embraced him, and showed him love and compassion beautifully.

God Did His Thing

It wasn't a coincidence…
It didn't need evidence
For us to be together…
A marriage license?! Foolishness!
God did his thing.
It didn't need a ring
Because that's not what bounded our souls…
God created us to be together…
Destined us to be one forever.
God did his thing.
He made me your queen and you my king…
It didn't need evidence…
God just did his thing…
It didn't need a ring.

Love is pure. Love is cure. Love is air. Love is fair. Love is me, love is you. Love is you and I. So, let's fly. Let our love touch the sky.

Love is the safety boat that takes you to a secure shore when life tries to hit you with its coming up and down waves.

He played on the sensitive strings of her soft heart
the best melodies ever. He chose her love to be
their song of forever. The tone was sad at the
beginning, but they changed it later, for love
always prevails. They caught each other's hands
and walked together to forever.

Let her fly. Let her be who she is. Many suffocated hearts cried in silence. Many broken spirits bled for losing their essence. Many weary souls were lost, wandering aimlessly, looking to regain their innocence. Let her be out of your tied chains. Let her be who she is.

Love leaves us no option.
Either we love to feel alive or we are dead souls.

When life wondered and questioned,
love comforted and answered.

Too long?
But it would be a chance for you to learn
the right from the wrong.

She breathed Love in a suffocated life. For it was and will always be her only savior. She missed no breath without telling him "I love you". She never regretted to sacrifice her life in the name of Love to see it alive. Therefore, she chose Love and made it her life.

He uttered the word "goodbye", recklessly. She raised her shaking hand and placed it on his lips. "You will remember me wherever you go", she challenged.

He smiled. Took her hand away and left.

He did his best to forget her and move on with his life by flying from one flower to another. His selfish plan was to take and never give. He knew there would be tears—but never his.

The clock ticked. The flaw in his plan became obvious. It was obvious that his heart could smile only with her. He tried to suppress those thoughts and deny the truth, but he smelled her fragrance wherever he went. Her specter followed him; he could see shadows of her here and there. He tried hard to run from the reality of her love until he realized that there was nowhere to go within himself where she would not be. He was running from himself.

Out of breath, he found himself knocking at the door of her soul. She opened, smiled, and placed a steady hand on his chest. Feeling the palpitations of his heart, she drew him in. She cuddled her love, welcoming him home in her soul. She was an unforgettable woman and a lesson learned; love always prevails.

She tried to kiss her memories of him away. Her lips said goodbye while her soul still longed for him. She couldn't take a step out of the cage her heart was in. She was sentenced to love him forever. She would live out her life in the depth of his soul. Her breaths can only come in his presence, so how will she live in his absence?

They wanted to break her spirit. But she opened
her heart widely. They tossed it with stones. It hurt
her badly. They stepped on her beautiful soul to
taint it. But she stood against them firmly. She was
an angel even in a world of evil. She chose mercy
and forgiveness. She was a shiny light in the world
of darkness.

She didn't want to think. She cleared her mind of the doubts that may lead her to his reality. She preferred to walk blindly in the darkness of the imagination and illusioned perfection. Because one bad thought may pull her to the depth of reality and make her let go of him instead of covering the bad thoughts about him.

Not everything can be fixed with "I am sorry".
Cold words can chill the feelings someone had for
you and freeze their heart. Think twice before
speaking, before you turn a lover's heart to ice.

Love can't be healed after wounds get sealed on the heart. Think before you act, because even when things fall deep and seem in bottom, one move arises them up again. They are never gone and vanish.

She dreamt, wished, and hoped to be a part in his life, but things between them fell apart. The thread of their destiny was ripped out. He couldn't be out of his dreamy bubble to meet her out there. Hopes shattered, but her faith strengthened. She believed in what was meant for her will surely be. She surrendered and walked away to an unknown destination. Maybe to where she would find stronger threads that can hold her one day to her fate.

She held burdens on her shoulders. But never paid heed to the pain she lived every day, since she knew the light in her would guide her to the right way. She knew she would heal her wounds, not with time but her will. And so, her hopes, dreams came out to light. Her smiles and laughs came again to life. She knew that life was not about what it wanted her to be, but what she wanted it to be.

Every one of us has a story to tell,
but not all of us can say it beautifully.

Once upon a time, there was a woman who life threw at her stones. She got hurt from all sides. She went right, but found everyone left. She went left, but found herself looking for her right. She felt lonely. But stood up bravely. She ran straight ahead to her destination. She didn't count what she left and missed behind. She planned for what she would find next after she woke up from a long tiring way. She is a timeless woman.

A yell of pain and regret shook her within but taught her how to be strong again. Her soul woke up. She could see the reality of things. Scars of the past wouldn't stop her from being who she wanted to be but reminded her of how she should be. She took the past as a learned lesson to build a solid bridge to her bright unbreakable future. She was a strong woman.

Time began running out from her, she thought. She kept counting from ten to zero. She pushed harder and harder to change. She had efforts to make up what was left. She kept looking behind. But whenever she looked at herself, she found out she was still at the same point. She changed her way again. She threw her past behind, and ejected every bad thought. She knew that Life wasn't about numbers to count, and not to look back to make up and fix. Life is to think forward when you walk forward, and then she could move on.

Woman are like flowers. They fade if they were used only for smelling the fragrance. They need to be taken care of, so they blossom in love and light beautifully.

His shadow followed her wherever she went. His fragrance she smelled here and there. Everything reminded her of him. His absence made a deep hole in her soul. She couldn't be whole. She kept running over his shadow 'til she realized it was an illusionary love. If he truly loved her, he would be there with her. If he loved her, he could never be a shadow, but a hand to catch hers firmly and walk together to their fate… She woke up. Looked at what was waiting for her to make her whole again… And then all the illusions came to conclusions.

Thinking to have this and that, and a few more of whatever, you keep running after things that run away from you, while ignoring something that is already in your hands. There is nothing wrong with wanting more as long as you can handle the frustration. So, the choice is yours. Stop chasing frustrations and spend more time appreciating the blessings you have already, before you turn back to see that what you turned your back on has run away from you too.

Falling is a means of growing.

Changes come with reasons.
Be some of the reasons for beautiful changes.

Sometimes, pain is good for us to move forward. Otherwise, we stay fighting for what is not for us and what we may never get, which is more painful.

The Quest

By Lourdes Alexander and Salima Mansouri

Salima

She threw the blame on life.

She thought she would get what she dreamed of when she counted from one to five.

She forgot that she had to strive.

She forgot that she had to love to taste life.

She roamed in the world of fantasies to find the key to her happy life.

She sought for a realm to dwell in her dreamy life.

She forgot Life would ask her to wake up to live and love.

Life hinted "Love is Me".

She found the secret key to her happy life.

She LOVED, for Love was the only way to bring her to Life.

Lourdes

She had beauty and brains, too.

But her life was yet another Cinderella story…

She became mature at a tender age.

She accepted responsibility with a positive attitude.

She never let a day sweep by without a smile.

She cherished every moment of her life.

She believed that after every dusk there was dawn.

Her wings, though clipped, but her spirits were never strong.

She weathered every storm that gave her a topsy-turvy ride;

Never gave up for she even defied Life.

Life had to surrender and bow down at her unfailing spirit,

Turning into reality every dream she once wished.

Her story was hopeless, but she was a ray of hope.

She even got her Love, for she was Love!

She ran away from her real world because life was severe with her. Therefore, she created a beautiful place for herself in her dreamy land. It was her peaceful space where she could imagine the life she couldn't have in reality. She saw that the world out of her world was dark. She denied it. She hoped so she could enhance the light she had within with her optimistic thoughts and dreams. And she surely could.

Her dreams would take her to a fairytale land, but she didn't want to live an unreal momentary happiness. She sees staying in the light of her reality as her being an awakened soul. Even in a breakable life, she is a brilliantly resilient woman.

Don't spend time trying to understand Life.
Sometimes it tells you lies when you need to hear
the truth. And sometimes it hurts you with the truth
when you need it to lie to you.

Sometimes, it feels like we have to hurt ourselves to heal others. Just like a candle has to burn and melt away, so it enlightens others' ways.

The ones who come new to your life are not responsible for mending your breaks. They should never be thought of as a cure. Cure yourself. Cure your injuries before giving them to others to heal.

Souls hold secrets that only eyes can reveal.

Be careful in your plans.
The way in is not always a way out.

She dreamt to be like a bird. Free to choose her way in her way. She chose the sky because she wanted to see the world as tiny as she could from above. And she is bigger than her worries. She could have a different view to the world. She was free because she freed her mind and soul before to float with her body here and there.

Get your mind off what has left from you and stay focused on what is left for you. Only then can you make a difference to yourself and others who are worth your time.

Embrace and love yourself. Your heart needs to feel you first. See with your heart, because beauty is a feeling.

Release your mind. Let go of any negativity it is chained to. Attach it to positivity. Then share it. Positivity is beautifully contagious. But it has to begin with you. AWAKEN THE LIGHT within you, and make the universal shift emanate from you. Your world is you, and what you make matter to you.

Leaving you? Stop yourself! Leave the baggage
you are carrying with you. Stop packing your past.
Live forward as you move forward, and free
yourself by embracing your new you.

Are you leaving soul, heart, and mind to your new
world? Or leaving your everything behind you, and
you are only the body who leaves? Make sure to
take all of you with you. Be the new you when it
didn't work out with the old you.

Don't be a prisoner of your thoughts. Free your mind by freeing it from the closed-minded thoughts that imprison you.

Bodies live Life. Souls live Light.

The relationship between love and life is exchangeable because we love to live and live to love.

Life is a balance of living. Either we take it too seriously and miss the joy in it, or we take the joy for granted and forget its value.

Imitation is a limitation. It puts a wall up around your imagination. Be unique in being yourself.

Appreciate yourself and get to know who you are, or others will be introducing you to you.

Leave the bitter, and live the sweet.
Leave the lies, and live your truth.
Leave the hatred, and live your love.
Life is all about what you leave and what you live.
Are you deciding to live it or leave it?

You are a soul disguised in a body.
Be yourself. Be your essence.

The dark clouds life set over your head can remain there if they like. The patience and faith you have in you and your need to feel happiness shower down on you will have you enjoying a dance in the rain.

Life is a constantly moving sea. We sometimes forget to swim with the current and fight against the waves, instead. But we have to float with Life to make it safely to peaceful shores.

Get out of your shell. You are deeper than that shallow cover. Break the chains that imprison your soul. Come out with the light in you and shine.

Life blames. Love forgives.

Eventually, you have to pay back what you have spent in life. It is as if it spins itself around again and pauses at a specific point in the past. A moment resets itself, and you restart living a moment you thought was gone and done. When this happens, be sure you are not living the bad experiences twice.

Life is the race being run.
Love is the breaths we take in between.

And yet there is no better touch than having your soul touched. The right place. The deepest. The sincerest.

Judge no one for their failings until you put
yourself in the same situation and think of what
you would have done. You may have made worse
decisions than they did in that instant.

Doubts are the shadow of insecurity.

The relationship between the body and the soul is limited and confining, but also temporary. Free your thoughts on this matter. The light in you will shine freely and live forever.

Those who never walked in darkness do not know their way to light.

The sense of love is to love with your essence.

Do not tamper with wounded hearts. Be gentle with them. Be careful not to open them forcefully or step on them randomly. You may be hurting more than healing. Teasing the wounds causes more bleeding.

It's true that life is not compassionate all of the time. But it is not a tough guy all the time. Catch it tenderly by the right hand and slowly walk with it. Because it is all about taking the time to understand it.

Life is not what you look behind to fix nor to what you look forward to expect. It is a momentary peaceful living.

Someone hurt you? Why are you carrying that cup
of pain with you? You didn't like its bitter taste
when it was served to you, so why would you give
it to others to taste. Throw the cup in the trash.
Take the bad taste in your mouth as a lesson
learned.

Do not fear taking a journey to the dark depths of
your soul to take a closer look at your dark side.
Darkness is a part of us. It is the only way that
leads us to our light.

Plant the seed of love in your heart and water it
with light from your soul. Then watch your soul
blossom in love and light.

Don't let your ego overcome the love in you. Since when has darkness ever overcome light?! Dig inside. Have a deep conversation with what disturbed your peace and threatens to destroy the beauty in you. Then demolish all ill feelings that stand against your passion, love, and light.

Excuse those whom life didn't show mercy. They have never tasted its sweetness. How do you expect them to give you what they have never gotten if you don't show them how to be merciful? Show them how to forgive themselves, so they can see beauty in life again!

Change any destination that takes you to the
unknown. Blind heart will have you wandering
aimlessly on an endless dark journey.

Deep eyes don't always tell the truth because they
sometimes have shallow views. But hearts see it
all.

Not all the periods will show the end of the story. There will be some in between endings. They will give you a chance to start new statements in your life; ones that will come with the conclusions you wish for.

Everything turns to nothingness in the absence of Love. Love is you, me, and all of us. Love is the universe.

Never wait for someone to come and put a crown on your head to make you a queen. Queens are Queens when they are born. It doesn't take a crown being worn.

Do not let the day leave you before leaving it with a smile. Life is too short to have a frown on its face. Karma is karma. Life will reciprocate what you send it.

Never look at yourself in the broken's eyes. They will never be a reflection of who you are because they will always have you see yourself as incomplete, for they miss in themselves trust and completeness.

Life spirals back on itself. We sometimes think we are running away from what we did, but Life will meet us again with "Hello, do you remember me?". Realize that it charges us for what we didn't pay, because nothing in Life is free.

Within her is a voice calling for freedom. Eager to build its own kingdom that no one shares and there are no cares. She wanted to be lonely again. Some would think she was insane. Some asked her who would save her from herself on the days of heavy rain. She didn't pay heed and freed herself from what had bounded her soul for so long. She felt what others don't feel is right is not necessarily wrong. Then she celebrated her freedom with a song, "I am not lonely. I am free to be me".

Life steals our unity. Only love gathers us and reunites our souls forever.

You can't recognize the greatness of things 'til you go deeper into them. Shallow sights come from narrow minds.

Believe in yourself. Greatness relies on how much you matter to you.

Don't blame Love because of what your hearts
have seen from those who call themselves lovers.
Love is innocent from hurt, deception, and lies.
Love is the purest and the greatest feeling ever
God gifted to us. Open your heart for the right
person and make it bleed with honesty and giving.

We don't have to hurt those who hurt us or deceive the ones who have deceived us. That was a reflection of who they are. That was their dark path they chose to walk on, not ours. Let's choose our own way of love and forgiveness. Because Light always overcomes darkness.

You will never know what freedom is 'til you let go of the pain keeping you in the chains that tie your feelings and limit your thinking. Freedom is a choice made from within.

Her eyes mesmerize. Her gaze to love and life will always rise. Her radiant smile is as beautiful as the first day of July. Her eyes never lie. I walked slowly through her soul, and through the heart I passed by. I felt an innocent girl inside of her. Her eyes never tell a lie.

She hoped, dreamed, and believed… but her
dreams went against her and what she wanted to
reach. Her unbreakable spirit flew unwillingly but
bravely to her forever destination.

She is not a body.
She is a forever illumination.

She fell and rose. She hurt unintentionally and was hurt. She made wrong decisions and right ones. She lived the polarities. She had a dark side, but her light overcame the bad in her. She loved herself. Accepted her truth. That what made her to look at herself as a perfectly imperfect woman. Because she lived perfections under the shadow of imperfections.

About The Author

Salima Mansouri, called "Papillon"; a word in French meaning Butterfly; is a teacher of French and English. Her friends and family called her "Papillon" for the reason of joy she brings wherever she lights up. Salima was born on the 22nd of March, 1983, in Batna, Algeria. She is also a writer and poet. She writes in the English language, although her first language was Arabic.

Writing for her is to vent out on herself and to challenge and be proud of who she is. It is also meant to invite and lead others to love life. Since there is always love inside of us, we will always win and feel alive. Although there is a sad touch in her writings, she opens the doors of hope and optimism at the end. Pain is a part of our life. We can't deny that.

Salima lived in a bubble, protected and loved by family. She has experienced a few things in this life but learned much from listening to others and caring about their problems!

Salima is very ambitious; a dreamer, persistent on success. Falling, according to her, means growing.

Her soul is still falling to grow up and call you soon to share her next work: a novel.